Jayne Flaagan

Husky Publishing
East Grand Forks, MN
email: djflaagan@gra.midco.net

Copyright © 2015 Jayne Flaagan
Cover Design © 2015 Jayne Flaagan

No part of this publication may be reproduced in whole or in part, or stored in a retrieval system, or transmitted in any form or by any means, electronic, mechanical, photocopying, recording or otherwise, without written permission of the author/publisher.

"The Four Children Who Were Very Good"
is dedicated to
my four special Godchildren,
for whom this book was written,
Winston, Zachariah, Audrey and Eleonoora

Jayne Flaagan grew up in North Dakota and made the big move to Minnesota many years ago. She lives with her husband and a goofy dog named Ella. She also has three grown children.

Flaagan has over 30 years of experience and education in Early Childhood Education. She has been writing for many years and receives much joy and satisfaction working in this genre. Flaagan writes the "Ella the Doggy" book series. She lives with her husband and a goofy dog named Ella. Her website is www.ellathedoggy.com and you can reach her at djflaagan@gra.midco.net.

Once upon a time, there were four children who lived in Grand Forks, ND.

Winston, Zach, Audrey and Noora were very good children!

These four children were especially good at art.

Noora, the baby of the family, liked to paint the kitchen floor.

Winston and Zach were good at making great designs on their clothes...

and Audrey was very good at making sure the living room door was kept bright and colorful when company came!

Winston, being the oldest, had to quickly get good at wearing many different hats.

As the first child, Winston was also very good about letting Mom and Dad take funny pictures of him...

and when he got older, he got very good at making himself look funny - without any help from Mom or Dad!

Zach, the second child, learned from his older brother that he should stay away from strangers,

so he only hugged strangers who were made of plastic...

and he only took candy from strangers when he had a VERY LARGE bag to fill! (and when his Mom and Dad were there)

Noora, the fourth child, had to become very good about all the extra attention she was given because she was the baby of the family ...and because she couldn't talk.

but mostly Noora was good at winning everyone's heart and just plain being cute.

By the time that fourth child came along, Zach became TERRIBLY good about combing his own hair...

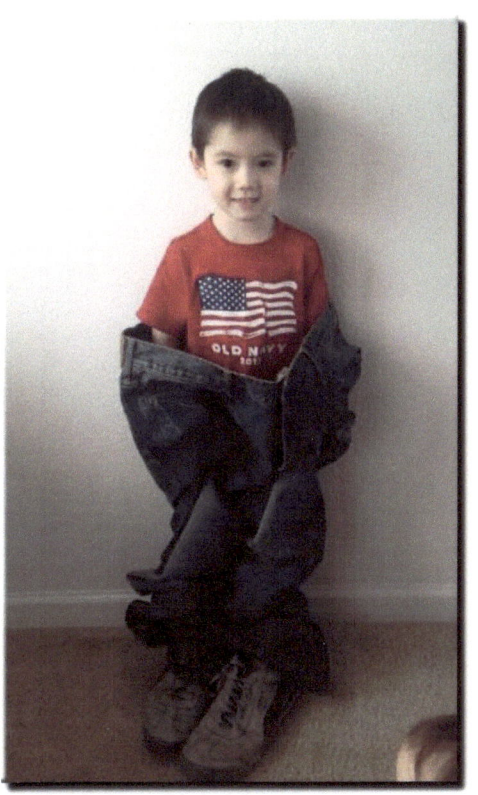

and getting dressed all by himself.

Oh - did we mention how cute
and loveable Noora was?

(We had to mention that twice because of how good she was at those things!)

These four children were also very good at showing their Mom and Dad how much they loved them...

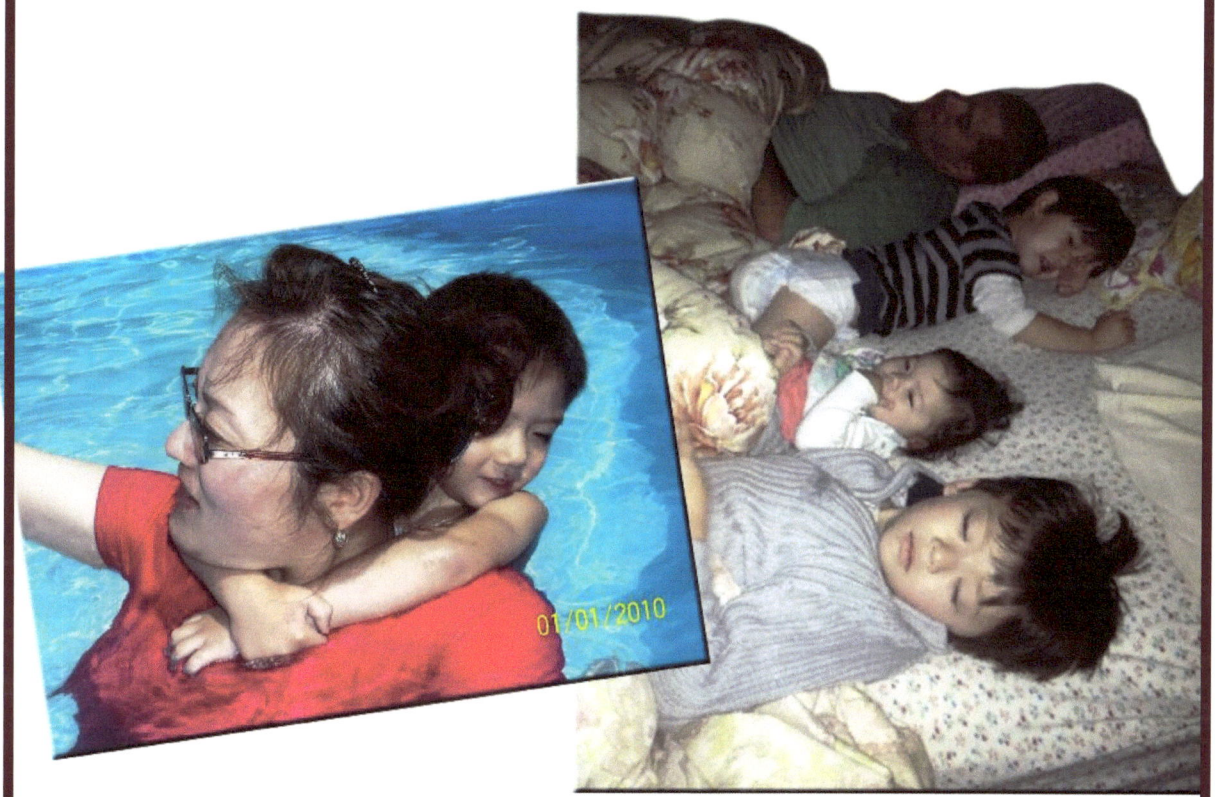

and just to prove it, they always did their best to make sure Mom and Dad were never alone for one single minute!

When the four siblings drove their vehicles, they were very good about not going over the speed limit...

What these four children were the best at was being special.

God makes every person wonderfully unique.

There never was and never will be another Winston, Zach, Audrey or Noora.

And that is really what makes all children ever created so very, very good.

Thank you for your purchase of "*The Four Children Who Were Very Good*."

Visit www.jayneflaagan.com. When you leave your name and email there, you will be sent a link to download a **FREE coloring book** of "*The Four Children Who Were Very Good!*"

As a subscriber, you will be notified when this author writes new books AND when you can download her Kindle books for FREE!

From time to time, you will also receive fun and useful information about books for children and other relevant information.

If you enjoyed this book, please copy and paste the following web address in your browser to leave a review: http://www.amazon.com/dp/B00Y63XD9M

Jayne Flaagan also writes a book series called "*Ella the Doggy*," stories about a real Husky with large, colorful photos. When you visit her web site at www.elladoggy.com and leave your name and email, you will receive numerous special gifts, including:

1. A link to receive a FREE audio book of "*Doggy's Busy Day*"

2. Emails letting you know when Ella's new books come out AND when FREE Kindle downloads of Ella's books are offered

3. FREE coloring pages of Ella to print and color

4. An entry into the monthly drawing for a FREE Ella the Doggy book. (Three winners will be selected each month).

Visit http://www.ellathedoggy.com

www.ingramcontent.com/pod-product-compliance
Lightning Source LLC
Chambersburg PA
CBHW041423060426
42444CB00031B/127